STILL MORE Jokes

compiled by J. Michael Shannon
illustrated by Diana L. Magnuson

created by The Child's World

CHILDRENS PRESS, CHICAGO

Library of Congress Cataloging in Publication Data
Shannon, J. Michael.
Still more jokes.

Summary: A collection of jokes on subjects such as history, math, science, animals, and famous people.
1. American wit and humor.   2. Wit and humor,
Juvenile.   [1. Jokes]   I. Magnuson, Diana, ill.
II. Child's World (Firm)   III. Title.
PN6163.S53   1986   818'.5402   85-27971
ISBN 0-516-01867-1

Copyright © 1986 by Regensteiner Publishing Enterprises, Inc.
All rights reserved. Published simultaneously in Canada.
Printed in the United States of America.
 6 7 8 9 10 11 12 R 93 92

TABLE OF CONTENTS

Introduction 4

Doctor, Doctor 6

Waiter, Waiter 11

About Animals 15

Around the House 18

Did You Hear the One About 21

About School 24

Daffy Definitions 28

Just Plain Silly 31

Still More Jokes 39

Introduction

Have you ever told a joke and no one laughed? That's a terrible feeling, isn't it? Don't worry. Everyone who tells jokes has experienced that embarrassing silence. The problem is that no one really knows why we laugh at jokes. Many great thinkers have studied this very idea.

Some say we laugh because the joke sets us up for a surprise. For example:

Boy 1: My dad has 500 men under him.
Boy 2: He must be a big executive.
Boy 1: No, he cuts the grass at a cemetery.

Others say we laugh because we put things together that don't normally belong together. Here is one example:

A man walked into the psychiatrist's office with a fried egg on his head, a strip of bacon over each ear, and two little sausages stuck in his nose. The doctor asked, "Can I help you?" The man replied, "No, I'm here about my brother."

Sometimes a joke is funny because it is told at just the right time and in the right situation. And sometimes a joke is funny because the joke teller has learned to tell the story in a humorous way. This could mean emphasizing a certain key word or words, using a different dialect or accent, speaking fast or slow, loud or soft.

So, there are probably lots and lots of different reasons why jokes are funny. And we're glad they are. Think how boring life would be if there were no jokes.

Many years ago a man who was known to be very wise said, "A cheerful heart is good medicine." When someone laughs, he feels better. So why not make others happy. Tell them a joke. You'll find many in **STILL MORE JOKES**.

Doctor, Doctor

Girl: Doctor, my brother has carrots growing out of his ears.
Doctor: How awful!
Girl: Yes, we planted potatoes.

Patient: Doctor, I just broke my glasses yesterday. Do I have to be examined all over?
Doctor: No, just your eyes.

Doctor: Can I take your pulse?
Patient: Why, don't you have one of your own?

Patient: Doctor, what's wrong with me?
Doctor: You're sick.
Patient: Mind if I get a second opinion?
Doctor: Sure, you're ugly, too.

Patient: It hurts when I make a fist. What should I do?
Doctor: Don't make a fist.

Woman: Doctor, my husband thinks he's a chicken.
Doctor: How long has he been like this?
Woman: Six months.
Doctor: Why didn't you come to me sooner?
Woman: Well, we would've, but we needed the eggs.

Freddy: You know, I've been seeing spots before my eyes.
Betty: Have you seen a doctor?
Freddy: No, just spots.

Patient: Doctor, my hair's falling out. Can you give me something to keep it in?
Doctor: How about a shoe box?

Patient: Doctor, I just swallowed some film. What should I do?
Doctor: I guess we'll have to wait and see if anything develops.

Woman: Doctor, you've got to help my husband; he chews his nails.
Doctor: That's not so bad, is it?
Woman: They're his toenails.

Jane went to see her doctor because she had a bad cold. The doctor said, "I want you to drink some orange juice after a hot bath."

Jane said, "Okay." Later she called her doctor. She said, "Doctor, I can't drink this orange juice."

"Why?" said the doctor.

"I don't have room after drinking the hot bath," she said.

Patient: What is black, has brown spots, and crawls?
Doctor: I give up. What?
Patient: Whatever it is, it's crawling on your arm.

Patient: Doctor, can you help me? I think I'm a dog. All the time, I think I'm a dog.
Doctor: How long have you felt like this?
Patient: Ever since I was a puppy.

Patient: Doctor, I sure hope I'm sick.
Doctor: You do?
Patient: Yes, I wouldn't want to feel this bad if I were well.

Patient: Doctor, I'm here because my husband says I need help.
Psychiatrist: What's the problem?
Patient: The problem is, I like pancakes.
Psychiatrist: That's not so bad.
Patient: But I really like pancakes.
Psychiatrist: So do I.
Patient: So there's nothing wrong with me?
Psychiatrist: Not at all.
Patient: Well, great! Maybe you can come and see my pancakes at the house. All of my closets are full of them.

Patient: Doctor, I keep having this ringing in my ear.
Doctor: Have you considered getting an unlisted ear?

Patient: Doctor, you've got to help me. Everything is backward.
Doctor: What do you mean?
Patient: My nose runs and my feet smell!

Doctor: I want you to go over to the window and stick your tongue out.
Patient: Why do you want me to do that?
Doctor: Because I'm mad at the guy across the street.

Nurse: Doctor, there's an invisible man in the lobby.
Doctor: Tell him I can't see him.

Patient: Doctor, Doctor, no one pays any attention to me.
Doctor: What did you say?

Patient: Doctor, Doctor, I'm so confused. I don't know if I'm a wigwam or a tepee.
Doctor: I think the problem is that you're just two tents (tense).

Patient: Doctor, do you think I should get my eyes checked?
Doctor: What's the matter? Don't you like them blue?

Waiter, Waiter

Customer: Waiter, do you serve crabs here?
Waiter: Yes, sir, we serve anyone. Sit right down.

Customer: Waiter, there's a fly in my soup.
Waiter: Not so loud. Everyone will want one.

Customer: Waiter, this coffee tastes like kerosene.
Waiter: I'm sorry, sir, you must have tea. Our coffee tastes like furniture polish.

Waiter: How did you find your steak, sir?
Customer: Well, it was hard, but I looked under a french fry, and there it was.

Customer: Waiter, what's this fly doing in my soup?
Waiter: It looks like the backstroke, sir.

Customer: Waiter, there's a dead fly in my soup.
Waiter: I'm sorry, sir, the heat must have killed it. I'll get you another.

Waiter: Ma'am, you can have anything on the menu.
Customer: Couldn't I have it on a plate?

Customer: Waiter, I can't eat this meal. Call the manager.
Waiter: It's no use, sir. He couldn't eat it either.

Customer: Waiter, this meal isn't fit for a pig.
Waiter: I'm sorry, sir, I'll bring out one that is.

Customer: Waiter, why is my donut crushed?
Waiter: Well, you said you wanted a donut and to step on it.

Customer: Waiter, there's a fly in my soup!
Waiter: That's not so bad.
Customer: What could be worse than that?
Waiter: Half a fly.

Customer: Waiter, there are two dead flies in my soup.
Waiter: That's funny. They were alive when I left the kitchen.

Customer: Does your chef have pig's feet?
Waiter: I don't know. I've never seen him with his shoes off.

Customer: Waiter, do you have frog's legs?
Waiter: No, it's just that my shoes are a little tight.

Customer: Waiter, are there eggs on the menu?
Waiter: Not any more. I wiped them off.

Customer: Waiter, there's a fly in my salad.
Waiter: That's nothing. You should see what's crawling on your bread.

Customer: Waiter, there's a spider in my soup.
Waiter: I'm sorry, sir, but we're all out of flies.

Waiter: Would you like me to cut your pizza in eight pieces or six pieces?
Customer: Better make it six. I don't think I could eat eight pieces of pizza.

About Animals

Mom: Did you give your goldfish some more water?
Son: No. He didn't finish what I gave him last week.

Freddy: Why does your dog scratch himself like that?
Betty: Because he's the only one who knows where it itches.

Man 1: I hear you play chess with your dog.
Man 2: Yes.
Man 1: He must be really smart.
Man 2: Not really. I usually beat him.

Boy: What kind of dog is that?
Girl: He's a police dog.
Boy: He sure doesn't look like one.
Girl: It's because he's in the secret service.

Tim: Did you put the cat out?
Terry: I didn't know he was on fire!

A little boy approached a dog who was both growling and wagging his tail. The little boy said, "I'd pet you, dog, but I don't know which end to believe."

Jenny: Jimmy, what are you doing?
Jimmy: Our dog is lost, so I'm putting a notice in the paper.
Jenny: Come on now, you know our dog can't read.

Sally: I think my dog can talk.
Jerry: What makes you think so?
Sally: When he walks over gravel, he says, "Ruff, ruff."

Mother Kangaroo: I sure hope it doesn't rain today.
Father Kangaroo: Why?
Mother Kangaroo: You don't know how bad it is when the kids have to play inside.

Rosemary: My dog is really mean.
Jill: What do you mean?
Rosemary: I have to tie a pork chop around my neck to get him to play with me.

Mark: My dog has no tail.
Melanie: Then how do you know when he's happy?
Mark: He stops biting.

Dog Catcher: Ma'am, can you help me? I'm looking for a dog with one eye.
Lady: Don't you think you'd have better luck if you used both eyes?

Becky: Did you call the zoo?
Tom: Yes, but the lion was busy.

Scott: I wonder what happens to old skunks?
Shirley: I guess they stop making scents.

A family was in a restaurant eating when the mother asked for a doggie bag to take the steak home in. The little boy shouted, "Oh boy, we're getting a dog!"

Beth: We got a cat, and I named him Theophilus.
Bob: Why did you name him that?
Beth: Because he's the awfulest (sic) looking cat I ever saw.

Around the House

Mother: Son, I want you to eat your spinach. It will put color in your cheeks.
Son: Who wants green cheeks?

Mother: Son, did you call your sister "stupid"?
Son: Yes.
Mother: You tell her you're sorry.
Son: Okay, sis, I'm sorry you're stupid.

Woman 1: Do you wake up grumpy in the morning?
Woman 2: No. He gets up all by himself.

Mother: Okay, son, wake up. Remember the early bird gets the worm.
Son: Yes, mother, but remember what the early worm got.

Father: You kids ought to appreciate how good you have it. When I was a kid, I had to live on a can of beans for a month.
Son: That must have been terrible, Dad. Did you fall off?

Billy: Mommy, mommy! My sister broke my truck.
Mother: How did she do that?
Billy: She broke it when I hit her on the head with it.

A man was walking in a dangerous part of town when four men tried to mug him. He put up a valiant effort. He fought so hard he nearly beat up all of the men. Finally, though, he gave out and in his pocket they found 75 cents. One of the muggers said, "I can't believe you put up such a fight for 75 cents." The man said, "I didn't. I thought you were going to get that $500 in my shoe."

Mother: Debbie, I wish you'd sneeze the other way.
Debbie: I didn't know there was another way to sneeze.

Father: Did you see in the paper that the average family now consists of 1½ children?
Samantha: I don't think that can be true.
Father: Why not?
Samantha: Because I've never seen half a child anywhere.

Father: Jerry, did you get a haircut (a hair cut)?
Jerry: No, dad, I got them all cut.

Joann: Mother, there's a man at the door with a bill.
Mother: Joann, you know only ducks have bills.

Henry: Are you having trouble with your memory?
Albert: I don't know. What makes you think so, George?
Henry: First, because my name is Henry; second, because I'm your brother; and third, we've talked about this ten times this week.
Albert: Talked about what?

Did You Hear the One About...

Freddy: Did you hear the one about the cross-eyed discus thrower?
Betty: No.
Freddy: He didn't set any records, but he sure kept everyone awake.

Freddy: Did you hear the one about the bed?
Betty: No.
Freddy: It's not made up yet.

Freddy: Did you hear the one about the ceiling?
Betty: No.
Freddy: Well, it's over your head.

Freddy: Did you hear the one about the rope?
Betty: No.
Freddy: Well, just skip it.

Freddy: Did you hear the one about the dirty window?
Betty: No.
Freddy: Well, you couldn't see through it anyway.

Did you hear the one about the egg?
It wasn't all it was cracked up to be.

Did you hear the one about the nose?
It never stopped running.

Did you hear the one about the weeds?
They covered a lot of ground.

Did you hear the one about the artist?
He always knew where to draw the line.

Did you hear the one about the light bulb?
Oh, it's a bright one.

Did you hear the one about the doctor?
It'll leave you in stitches.

Did you hear the one about the pickle?
It's a real dilly.

Did you hear the one about the explosion in the glue factory?
It was a sticky situation.

Did you hear the one about the ghost?
He's out of sight.

Did you hear the one about the old magician?
He's up to the same old tricks.

Did you hear the one about the peacock?
It's a beautiful tail (tale).

Did you hear the one about the farmer who fell in his pasture?
He went on a field trip.

Did you hear the one about the nearsighted snake?
He fell in love with a garden hose.

About School

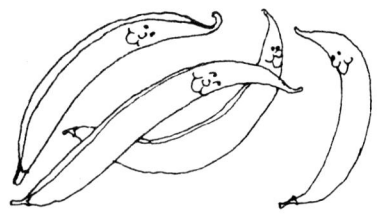

Teacher: Billy, why did you say that people are vegetables?
Billy: Because you told us we are all human beans.

Freddy: I heard that you don't like school.
Betty: Well, I don't mind school so much. It's just the principal of the thing.

Son: Dad, look. I got an "F" on my report card. Aren't you proud?
Dad: Why should I be proud?
Son: With a grade like that I couldn't possibly be cheating.

Teacher: Jimmy, why can't you get here on time? You're always late!
Jimmy: It's not my fault. There's a sign out front that says, "Slow, school ahead," so I had to slow down.

Student: Teacher, I don't think I deserved an "F" on this test.
Teacher: Neither do I, but that's the lowest grade I could give you.

Teacher: Sally, what's the English channel?
Sally: I don't know. I don't think it's on my T.V.

Billy: Hey, Willy, I heard that you were out of school yesterday.
Willy: Yes, I was out for sickness.
Billy: You don't look too bad to me.
Willy: I wasn't sick. The teacher was sick of me.

Teacher: Okay, Billy, how do you spell farm?
Billy: E-i-e-i-o.

Teacher: Willy, I wish you'd pay a little attention.
Willy: Teacher, don't you know by now I pay as little attention as possible?

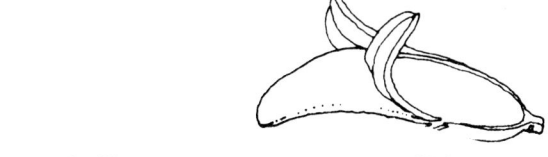

Teacher: Sally, I want you to spell banana.
Sally: B-A-N-A-N-A-N-A-N-A.
Teacher: No, that's wrong.
Sally: I'm sorry. I know how to spell it. I just don't know when to stop.

Teacher: Johnny, what would life have been like if Edison had not invented the light bulb?
Johnny: I guess we'd all have to watch T.V. in the dark.

25

Teacher: What did Julius Caesar say when he was stabbed?
Billy: "OUCH!"

Teacher: Carol, I understand you missed school yesterday.
Carol: No, Ma'am, I didn't miss it at all.

Teacher: Donnie, do you have trouble making up your mind?
Donnie: Well, yes and no.

Teacher: Is it proper to answer a question with a question?
Student: Why not?

Teacher: Terry, what's a Grecian urn?
Terry: I guess it depends on his job.

Teacher: Stephen, spell Mississippi.
Stephen: The river or the state?

Teacher: Todd, what are you going to be when you get out of school?
Todd: I'm afraid... an old man.

Teacher: I want it so quiet in here that I'll be able to hear a pin drop.
Student: (After a long silence): Well, where's the pin?

Teacher: Ben, I hope I didn't see you looking on someone else's paper.
Ben: I hope you didn't see me do it either.

Teacher: Tom, how do you know that the earth is round?
Tom: I never said that it was.

Rob: My sister is such a brain. She studies all the time.
Lucy: She can't study all the time.
Rob: Oh, yeah? She eats alphabet soup so she can read while she eats.

Daffy Definitions

TRICYCLE—a tot rod.

COCONUT—A bowling ball that forgot to shave.

DIPLOMA—"De" guy "dat" fixes "de" pipes.

BOYCOTT—Where a boy sleeps on a camp out.

BIGAMIST—A giant fog.

FARMER—A man outstanding in his field.

REINDEER—A horse with a T.V. antenna.

RAISIN—A worried grape.

BUCCANEER—A high price to pay for corn.

DEBATE—The stuff you catch fish with.

CAMELOT—A place to park your camel.

DENIAL—A river in Egypt.

ECLIPSE—What a barber does.

PARADOX—Two doctors.

CARTOON—A song sung by an automobile.

DECEIT—A place to sit down.

AROMA—A person who wanders around.

DUST—Instant mud.

SUNTAN—Organized freckles.

APPEAL—The skin of a fruit.

REPEAL—Something you can't do to a banana.

RINGLEADER—The referee in a boxing match.

FOOTBALL GAME—A group of people needing exercise watching a group of people needing rest.

VITAMIN—What you should do when a friend comes to the door.

CASTANET—One way to catch fish.

BREAD—Raw toast.

Just Plain Silly

Betty: Would you join me in a cup of tea?
Freddy: Well, I would, but I don't think we would fit.

Dad: Freddy, have you finished your chores?
Freddy: No, sir.
Dad: Now, Freddy, remember hard work never hurt anyone.
Freddy: I know. Dad, I just don't want to be the first.

Mom: Did you finish filling the salt shaker?
Freddy: No.
Mom: Why?
Freddy: It's so hard to get all that salt down in the little holes.

Man on a plane: Stewardess, remember when you gave me that gum for my ears?
Stewardess: Yes, didn't it work?
Man: It sure did, but now how do I get the gum out of my ears?

Man: Can you come down and help me get into my car? The doors are locked, and the key is in the ignition.
Locksmith: Sure. I'll get down there as soon as I can.
Man: Could you hurry? It's beginning to rain, and the top is down.

A boy showed up at his troop meeting with a black eye.
Scoutmaster: How did you get that black eye?
Boy Scout: I helped a lady cross the street.
Scoutmaster: That doesn't tell me how you got your black eye.
Boy Scout: She didn't want to go.

The T.V. networks had come to the home of a woman turning 115 years old. They asked her, "To what do you attribute your long life?" She said, "The fact that I haven't died yet."

A man came to court complaining he had gotten a ticket he didn't deserve. He said to the judge, "I don't know why they gave me this ticket. There was a sign next to the space that said, 'FINE FOR PARKING.'"

The town librarian got a call in the middle of the night. "What time do you open in the morning?" asked the voice on the phone.
She said, "Eight o'clock." The voice on the other end of the phone said, "That's the earliest, eight o'clock?" She said, "Yes. Why are you so concerned about getting in?"
The voice said, "I don't want to get in. I want to get out."

Freddy: My uncle has 500 men under him.
Betty: Is he a big executive?
Freddy: No, he cuts the grass at a cemetery.

Mother: Billy, answer the door.
Billy: Okay. Hello, door.

Freddy: Hey, Betty. What are you doing?
Betty: I'm writing my brother a letter.
Freddy: Why are you writing so slow?
Betty: My brother can't read fast, silly.

Betty: Freddy, where were you born?
Freddy: I was born in Kentucky.
Betty: What part?
Freddy: All of me was born there.

A young soldier was training to jump out of a plane with a parachute. They gave him all the necessary instructions on how to pull the rip-cord and told him that there would be a truck to meet him on the ground. After he jumped out of the plane, the first chute didn't work. He tried the reserve chute, and it didn't work either. He said, "Well, with my luck, I bet the truck won't be there either."

There were once two counterfeiters. They made a mistake and printed some fake $21 dollar bills. One of the men said, "I know a place where the clerk is so stupid I think I could give him those bills and he would accept them."

They went down to a little store and walked in and bought a cup of coffee. One counterfeiter said to the storekeeper, "Can you change a $21 dollar bill?"

The storekeeper said, "Sure, will three $7's be all right?"

Some men in a small town used to tease a little boy by offering him a dime or a nickel. He always chose the nickel because it was bigger. They would laugh and make fun of him. Finally, a couple said to the little boy, "Do you know what a dime is worth?"

The little boy said, "Ten cents." They said, "Do you know what a nickel is worth?" He said, "Yes, five cents." They said, "Then why do you let those men fool you?" He said, "If I ever take the dime, they'll quit trying it on me."

Man speaking to construction worker: Well, what are you all up to? Putting up a new building?
Construction Worker: Well, yes. They usually don't let us put up an old one.

Henry: I heard your son is eight years old.
Ben: Yes, he is.
Henry: How could you have a child that age?
Ben: He wasn't that age when we had him.

Rick: Our dog is like a member of the family.
Fred: Oh, yeah, which one?

Robber: All right, you, stick 'em down!
Victim: Don't you mean stick 'em up?
Robber: No wonder I haven't gotten anything!

Lady: Am I too late for the garbage?
Garbage Man: No, ma'am. Step right in.

Chris: Did I tell you about my grandfather? He raises cows?
Mark: Boy, he must really be strong.

Vicky: We got a brand new bike for my brother.
Pat: Oh, that sounds like a fair trade.

Mike: I wish I had enough money to buy the Empire State Building.
Chris: What would you do with the Empire State Building?
Mike: Nothing, I just wish I had enough money to buy it.

Visitor: Can I catch a bus here?
Old Man: I'm sorry, but I just don't think you are strong enough to catch a bus, young fellow.

Lucy: I'm having trouble seeing at night.
Larry: Then why don't you try going to night school?

Bill: I've got a new invention for instant hard-boiled eggs.
Jeff: What do you do?
Bill: I keep the chicken in hot water.

Lynn: What are you doing standing on your head in the kitchen?
Janet: I'm making an upside-down cake.

Lenny: Boy, I've got to remember to buy a fishing pole before election day.
Cindy: Why?
Lenny: Because they told me I'll have to cast a ballot.

Lady: Am I in time for the garbage?
Garbage Man: Sure, have some.

A lawyer was in his office for his first day of work. He heard footsteps coming down the hall. Wanting to look busy, he picked up the phone and pretended to talk to a client on the other end. He said, "Oh, yes, I can take care of that. I've been highly trained in that area." As a man entered the room, the lawyer looked up from the phone and said, "Can I help you?" The man said, "Yes, I'm here to hook up your phone."

Sharon: What are you doing jumping up and down?
Steve: I took some medicine that said, "Shake Well Before Using," but I forgot to shake it up.

William: Has it been hot on the farm this year?
Tom: Yes, it's been so hot that we raised baked potatoes.

A man had been pestered by a mouse so long that he was desperate. He set up a mousetrap, and not having any real cheese, put a picture of cheese in the mousetrap. The next day he found that the trap had been sprung, but inside the mousetrap was a picture of a mouse.

Betty: Do I seem grumpy today?
Fran: No, why?
Betty: I didn't get a chance to take a nap yesterday.
Fran: Why was that?
Betty: I slept right through it.

Carol: Why don't you answer the phone?
Terry: Why should I? It's not ringing.
Carol: Why wait 'til the last minute?

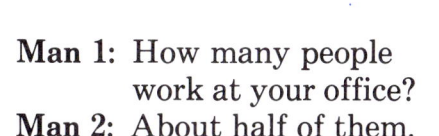

Still More Jokes

Man 1: How many people work at your office?
Man 2: About half of them.

Man 1: Do you have a criminal lawyer in this town?
Man 2: We think so, but we haven't caught him at anything yet.

Man 1: How many great men were born in this town?
Man 2: None, only babies.

Man 1: Have you lived in this town all your life?
Man 2: Not yet, I haven't.

Man 1: Did you call me stupid?
Man 2: Yes.
Man 1: Those are fighting words where I come from.
Man 2: Oh, yeah?
Man 1: It's a good thing we're not where I come from.

Police Officer: Sir, don't you know this is a one-way street?
Driver: But officer, I was only driving one way.

Everything was going fine on the cruise ship until a young girl fell off. She began to scream, "Help me, help me!" An old gentleman flew through the air and into the water. He flailed away and swam to the girl and brought her back to the boat. Everyone was amazed. Someone asked him, "What I want to know is, how you managed to get up enough courage to jump in the water and save that girl?" The man said, "What I want to know is, who pushed me in the water?"

Coach: Son, have you done much pitching before?
Pitcher: Yes, I have five pitches.
Coach: What are they?
Pitcher: Fastball, a curve, a slider, a knuckler, and the one that gets all the way to the catcher.

Airline Pilot: Well, I have good news and bad news for you. The bad news is we don't know where we're going. The good news is we're making great time!

Judge: All right, young men, why were you brought here?
First Man: For throwing peanuts in the lake.
Judge: That's not so bad. What about you?
Second Man: I'm here for throwing peanuts in the lake.
Judge: That seems pretty harmless. What about you?
Third Man: I'm Peanuts.

Tim: Did everyone like your home movie?
Todd: They were glued to their seats.
Tim: So that's the only way you could get them to see it?

Lynn: I think my boyfriend just insulted me.
Cindy: What did he say?
Lynn: He said I looked like a million.
Cindy: What's wrong with that?
Lynn: Who wants to be all green and wrinkled?

Dave: Do you think I'm too heavy?
Henry: Why do you ask?
Dave: I just weighed myself on a scale, and it said, "One at a time, please."

Dan: I'm going on a diet.
Vern: For what?
Dan: I want to win the no belly prize.

Man 1: I heard your new business made you a millionaire.
Man 2: Yes. Before I went in this business, I had five million.

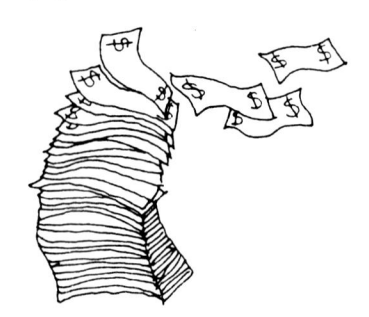

Woman looking at painting: This painting is awful. What would make it look better?
Woman 2: A long distance.

Two men were fishing, and they saw a young man who was catching fish every time he put his line in the water. They asked him what his secret was, and he just mumbled. They asked him a second time, and again he mumbled. Finally they insisted, "Please, tell us your secret."

The young boy took a long swallow and said, "You have to keep your worms warm."

Lucy: Yesterday, I was down in the dumps.
Mary: Oh, yeah? What did you find there?

Jim: You know, I think I have a concrete mind.
Jeannette: What makes you think that?
Jim: It's permanently set and all mixed up.

Jenny: Do you know how to paddle a canoe?
Jill: Sure I can, canoe?

A man was taking his small child shopping with him in the grocery store. The child was crying at the top of his lungs. The man kept saying, "Take it easy, Bernie, stay calm, Bernie." No matter what the child did, he simply looked down and said, "Take it easy, Bernie. Stay calm, Bernie." A woman thought he must be the most patient man alive.

"I'm going to congratulate him," she said. She went over to the man. "I really must commend you. You are so patient with little Bernie."

The man said, "His name is John. I'm Bernie."

Lenny: I heard that your father went on the roller coaster.
Jenny: That's right.
Lenny: Why?
Jenny: Because he's bald.
Lenny: What did that have to do with it?
Jenny: He heard that riding on that roller coaster was a hair-raising experience.

Jerry: Boy, when I was a kid, I had it tough. I had to wear hand-me-downs.
Jim: That's not so bad. So did I.
Jerry: Yes, but you had brothers. I only had sisters.

John: Did I tell you that my uncle is a boxer?
Dave: Is he good?
John: Yes, he's on a winning streak.
Dave: How many has he won?
John: One in a row.

Laura: I heard you just came back from vacation. How was it?
Linda: It was terrible! Our room was so small.
Laura: How small was it?
Linda: Well, when I went to sleep, I had to sleep with my feet out the window.

Jill: Mommy, is daddy going bald?
Mom: No, he's just getting a little tall for his hair.

Daryl: Paul, did you notice that you have one green sock and one brown sock on?
Paul: That's funny, I have another pair just like that at home.

Mark: My girl friend really got mad at me yesterday.
Ted: Didn't you compliment her like I told you?
Mark: Yes, I told her she had a face that would stop a clock.
Ted: There's your mistake. I told you to say that looking at her made time stand still.

Barbara: Do you know that I haven't slept in days?
Brenda: How terrible.
Barbara: It's not so bad. I sleep at night.

Charles: Have you noticed that our dog has affectionate eyes?
Diana: Yes, they're always looking at each other.

Mom: Son, I'm tired of you reaching for things across the table. Don't you have a tongue?
Son: Yes, but my arm is longer.

Bill: May I be frank with you for a moment?
Bob: Why don't you want to be yourself?

Joan: Is there a cure for love at first sight?
Pam: Yes, a second look.

David: I think my mother is way too neat.
Jane: Aren't you exaggerating a bit?
David: I don't think so. She gift wraps the garbage before she sets it out.

Charles: When I grow up, I want to be a professional bowler.
Charlene: Well, that ought to be right down your alley.

Donna: My crazy brother took a mirror to bed.
Christine: Why did he do that?
Donna: He wanted to see what he looks like when he's asleep.

Tom: Something really weird happened to me the other day.
Ron: What was that?
Tom: I picked up a seashell to listen to it, and I got a busy signal.

Tony: Can you keep a secret?
Ernest: Yes, but the people I tell it to can't.

Joe: How did you get that black eye?
Moe: I had to fight for it.

LOCUST GROVE ELEM. LIBRARY

T 004352

Donated in memory of
Wilton Hunter Talley &
Elizabeth Almond Talley
By Julia Talley Draucker
January, 1993